Before Religion

Book 1

FROM THE LAST BOOK OF GOD

Organized and translated by

Yassir Rousan

All interpretations here are my own. Any error lies solely with me.

Yassir Rousan

Contents

Introduction

This translation draws from the first five years of the final revelation bestowed upon the Prophet Muhammad over 1,600 years ago. At its heart, the message explores the fundamental nature of God, the creation of humanity and the universe, the purpose of life, and the accountability of everyone for their actions. It places profound emphasis on learning, as showed by its opening verse: "Learn! About your Lord, who created." Through knowledge, humanity uncovers the unknown and deepens its connection to the divine through His own words.

The text portrays God as the Lord of all worlds, the Most Merciful, the Sovereign of the Day of Judgment, and the Creator who fashions everything in its finest form. Described as the Most Generous and possessing boundless strength, God is eternal, singular, and without equal—neither begotten nor begetting, with no son or partner. He encompasses all that is seen and unseen, offering guidance to humanity. His unique name is a testament to His oneness.

A clear distinction is made between those who believe and those who reject the truth. Believers—characterized by their good deeds, commitment to truth, tolerance, and self-purification—strive for a "pleasant life" and the eternal reward of "paradise" or "gardens," where boundless blessings await. In contrast, those who deny the truth, show ingratitude, or commit evil are warned of dire consequences—facing the "great fire," "flaming fire," or "hell," where they will endure hardship and distress. The text vividly depicts the Day of Judgment as a moment of cosmic upheaval, when the earth will quake, mountains will crumble, stars will fade, and every soul will be judged according to their deeds.

Al-Alaq (*Surah 96*)

1. Learn! In the name of your Lord who created.
2. He created humans from a clinging shape, implantation of an embryo.
3. Learn! Your Lord is the most generous.
4. He taught us how to connect things together.
5. That's how humans learned what they did not know.

Al-Muddaththir (*Surah 74*)

1. Hey, you, under heavy sheets!
2. Wake up and give warning!
3. Acknowledge your Lord is the greatest.
4. Purify your clothes.
5. Leave your doubts and worries away.
6. Do not be overwhelmed by the task.
7. For your Lord, be patient.
8. And when the trumpet sounds off,
9. That will be a day of distress.
10. The disbelievers will have no ease.

Al-Masad (*Surah 111*)

1. Damn the hand of Abu Lahab, and damned is he.
2. For neither his wealth nor what he earned will help him.
3. He will be burned in the flaming fire.
4. And so will his wife, the firewood carrier,
5. With a palm-fiber rope around her neck.

Al-Takwir (*Surah 81*)

1. When the sun is folded,
2. When the stars are dimmed,

3. When the mountains are set in motion,
4. When pregnant camels are abandoned,
5. When wild beasts are herded together,
6. When the seas boil over,
7. When souls are reunited with their bodies,
8. When the baby girl buried alive is asked
9. For what sin she was killed,
10. When the records of deeds are spread open,
11. When the sky is scrubbed away,
12. When hell is made to blaze
13. And paradise brought near,
14. Every soul will know then what it has done.
15. I swear by the planets
16. That appear and disappear,
17. By the night that descends,
18. And by the dawn that softly breathes.
19. It is the speech of a noble messenger
20. Who possesses strength and access to the Lord of the throne
21. Obeyed and trusted.
22. Your companion is not mad.
23. He did see him clearly on the horizon.
24. He did not make this up.
25. And this is not the words of an outcast devil.
26. So where will you go?
27. It is only a reminder for both worlds,
28. For those among you who choose to be straight.
29. And the only reason you can choose freely is because God allowed it this way. He is the Lord of both worlds.

Al-A'laa (*Surah 87)*

1. Repeat your Lord's highest name.
2. The one that designed and executed,
3. Who estimated and guided,
4. Who brought out the grazing grass,
5. Then transformed it into bare shell.

6. We will teach it to you in a way where you will not forget.
7. Unless God wishes otherwise. He knows what's in the open and what's hidden.
8. We will ease your way.
9. So remind if reminding will help.
10. The ones with a conscience will remember.
11. And it will be ignored by the wicked,
12. Who will be burned in the great fire,
13. Where they will neither die nor live.
14. Successful is he who purifies himself.
15. And by recalling his Lord's name, he prays.
16. Yet you prefer this lower life,
17. Even though the next life is better and everlasting.
18. All this is mentioned in the earlier scriptures,
19. The scriptures of Abraham and Moses.

Al-Lail (*Surah 92*)

1. By the enshrouding night,
2. By daybreak,
3. And his creation of male and female,
4. Your goals differ greatly.
5. Whoever gives and is aware
6. And accepts without pressure,
7. We shall lead him toward ease.
8. But the one that's stingy, who thinks he can do without God,
9. And denies goodness,
10. We shall lead him toward hardship.
11. His wealth will not help him as he is perishing.
12. Our part is to provide guidance.
13. And for Us belongs the end and the beginning.
14. So I am warning you of a raging fire
15. In which none but the wicked will burn.
16. The one that denies and walks away.
17. But the one that's conscious of God will be spared.
18. The one that gives part of his wealth to purify it,

19. Not to return a favor to anyone,
20. But for the sake of his Lord's face, the Highest.
21. And he will be content.

Al-Fajr (*Surah 89*)

1. By the big bang,
2. By the timeline,
3. By the creation of protons and neutrons,
4. And by the passing darkness,
5. This oath is for the rational one.
6. Have you seen what your Lord did to Ad
7. Of Iram, the city of pillars?
8. Whose likeness has never been created in all the land?
9. And Thamud, who carved out rocks in the valley?
10. And the Pharaoh with the pyramids?
11. They exploited the countries
12. And increased corruption there.
13. Your Lord dealt them a quick blow.
14. Your Lord is always watching.
15. So when the human is tested by his Lord with honor and abundances, he says, "My Lord has honored me."
16. But when he is tested by the restriction of his livelihood, he says, "My Lord has humiliated me."
17. No indeed! You do not respect the orphan.
18. You do not urge each other to feed the poor.
19. You consume inheritance greedily.
20. And you love money with passion.
21. No indeed! When the earth is pounded to dust, pounded and pounded,
22. When your Lord comes with the angels, rank upon rank,
23. When hell on that day was brought near, on that day man will remember. But what good will that be to him?
24. He will say, "I wish I had provided for my future life."
25. On that day, no one will punish as He punishes,
26. And no one will bind as He binds.

27. Oh, you calm soul,
28. Return to your Lord, pleased and content.
29. Enter among my worshippers
30. And enter my garden.

Al-Dhuhaa (*Surah 93*)

1. By the morning brightness
2. And by the night when it grows still,
3. Your Lord has not said goodbye, nor did he leave.
4. And the future will be better for you than the past.
5. Your Lord will give you so you will be content.
6. Did He not find you an orphan and shelter you?
7. Did He not find you lost and guided you?
8. Did He not find you in need and made you self-sufficient?
9. So do not be cruel to orphans.
10. Do not scold the one who asks for help.
11. And tell about the blessings of your Lord.

Al-Sharh (*Surah 94*)

1. Did We not relieve your heart?
2. And lifted your burden
3. That weighed so heavily on your back?
4. And raise your status?
5. For sure, with hardship comes ease.
6. With hardship comes ease.
7. When you are done with your task, give attention
8. And turn to your Lord with love.

Al-Asr (*Surah 103*)

1. By the passing of time,
2. Human is a complete failure,

3. Except for those who believe, do what's right, encourage the truth, and encourage tolerance.

Al-Aadiyaat (*Surah 100*)

1. By the heavy breathing of horses
2. And the visible sparks made by their hooves
3. That charge in the early morning,
4. Raising a cloud of dust,
5. Plunging into the midst of the enemy,
6. Human is ungrateful to his Lord.
7. And he is witness to that.
8. He is truly excessive in his love of money.
9. Does he not know when the contents of graves are out?
10. When their secrets are revealed?
11. Their Lord on that day is an expert with them.

Al-Kawthar (*Surah 108*)

1. We have given you plenty.
2. So pray to your Lord and sacrifice.
3. It is the one that hates you who has been cut off.

Al-Takaathur (*Surah 102*)

1. You're so distracted by striving for more.
2. Till you visit the graves,
3. Indeed you will know.
4. And indeed you will know.
5. If you only knew for sure,
6. You will see hell.
7. Then you will see it for sure.
8. And you will be asked, on that day, about your good life.

Al-Maa'un (*Surah 107*)

1. Have you seen the one that denies his debt?
2. It is he who pushes aside the orphan
3. And does not encourage feeding the needy.
4. Great tragedy to those who pray,
5. The ones who neglect their connection,
6. Those who put on the appearance
7. But forbid common kindness.

Al-Kaafiroon (*Surah 109*)

1. Say, "Oh, you who deny,
2. "I do not worship what you worship,
3. "And you don't worship what I worship.
4. "I will never worship what you worshipped,
5. "And you will not worship what I worship.
6. "You have your debt to pay, and I have mine."

Al-Fil (*Surah 105*)

1. Have you seen what your Lord did to the army with the elephants?
2. Didn't he totally destroy their plan?
3. By sending on them ranks of Ababeel birds,
4. Throwing them with pellets of hard-baked clay,
5. It turned them into wasted garbage.

Al-Falaq (*Surah 113*)

1. Say, "I seek refuge with the Lord of fission (the splitting of the atom).
2. "From the harm of what He created.
3. "The harm in the coming of darkness.
4. "The harm in the magic spells.
5. "The harm in the envious when he envies."

Al-Naas (*Surah 114*)

1. Say, "I seek refuge with the Lord of people.
2. "The king of people.
3. "The God of people.
4. "From the harm of the sneaky whisperer,
5. "Who whispers into the foreheads of people,
6. "Among jinn and people."

Al-Iklhaas (*Surah 112*)

1. Say, "He is the one God,
2. "The eternal God.
3. "He does not have a son, nor was He born.
4. "And He has no equals."

Al Fatiha (*Surah 1*)

1. Thank God, Lord of both worlds.
2. Al Rahman, the Most Merciful,
3. In control of Payback Day.
4. We worship only You and seek help from You.
5. Guide us to the straight path,
6. The path of those You blessed, not of those who You are angry with nor of those who lost the way.

Al Rahman (*Surah 55*)

1. Al Rahman
2. Taught the Quran,
3. Created human,
4. Taught him spoken language.

5. The sun and the moon run their course.
6. The plants and the trees submit.
7. He raised the sky and set the balance.
8. So you must not mess with the balance.
9. Give out the right amounts and don't skim off the top.
10. He prepared earth for His creatures,
11. With its fruits and palm trees with dates,
12. Its grain and fragrant plants.
13. So which of your Lord's blessings do you deny?
14. He created man out of clay, like pottery.
15. And He created jinn out of fusion of fire.
16. So which of your Lord's blessings do you deny?
17. The Lord of the double sunrise and Lord of the double sunset.
18. So which of your Lord's blessings do you deny?
19. He merged river to sea.
20. Yet there is a barrier between them they do not cross.
21. So which of your Lord's blessings do you deny?
22. Pearls and morganite come from it.
23. So which of your Lord's blessings do you deny?
24. His are the floating ships like flags on the horizon.
25. So which of your Lord's blessings do you deny?
26. Everyone on it will perish,
27. Except for the majestic and honorable face of your Lord.
28. So which of your Lord's blessings do you deny?
29. Everyone in heaven and on earth is asking his help every day with a different matter.
30. So which of your Lord's blessings do you deny?
31. We shall attend to you heavyweight influencers.
32. So which of your Lord's blessings do you deny?
33. You jinn and humans, if you can pass through the realms of heaven and earth, do so. You will not be able to without Our authority.
34. So which of your Lord's blessings do you deny?
35. A flash of fire and copper will be released upon you, and no one will come to your aid.
36. So which of your Lord's blessings do you deny?
37. When the sky cracks, it will look like a painted rose.
38. So which of your Lord's blessings do you deny?

39.On that day, neither humans nor jinn will be asked about their sins.
40.So which of your Lord's blessings do you deny?
41.The criminal will be marked and dragged by their foreheads and their feet.
42.So which of your Lord's blessings do you deny?
43.This is the hell the criminals deny.
44.They will be exposed to it and its steaming heat.
45.So which of your Lord's blessings do you deny?
46.Those who fear facing their Lord get two gardens.
47.So which of your Lord's blessings do you deny?
48.With shading branches.
49.So which of your Lord's blessings do you deny?
50.With a pair of flowing springs.
51.So which of your Lord's blessings do you deny?
52.With every kind of fruit in pairs.
53.So which of your Lord's blessings do you deny?
54.Lying down over silk woven fabric within easy-to-reach fruit.
55.So which of your Lord's blessings do you deny?
56.Within them are companions with modest gaze, untouched before by human or jinn.
57.So which of your Lord's blessings do you deny?
58.They're like rubies and pearls.
59.So which of your Lord's blessings do you deny?
60.Shall the reward of goodness be anything but good?
61.So which of your Lord's blessings do you deny?
62.There are two more gardens below these two.
63.So which of your Lord's blessings do you deny?
64.Both of luscious green.
65.So which of your Lord's blessings do you deny?
66.With a pair of gushing springs.
67.So which of your Lord's blessings do you deny?
68.With fruits, palms, and pomegranate.
69.So which of your Lord's blessings do you deny?
70.There are lots of great goods.
71.So which of your Lord's blessings do you deny?
72.Companions sheltered in tents.
73.So which of your Lord's blessings do you deny?

74. Untouched before by human or jinn.
75. So which of your Lord's blessings do you deny?
76. They will all sit on green cushions and fine carpets.
77. So which of your Lord's blessings do you deny?
78. Blessed is your Lord's name, full of majesty and honor.

Al Najm (*Surah* 53)

1. By the shooting star,
2. Your friend did not go astray, nor was he deluded.
3. And he is not speaking on his own.
4. It is nothing but a revelation
5. Taught by a superpower.
6. This superpower revealed himself
7. On the highest horizon.
8. And then he came closer
9. Until he was two bow-lengths away or even closer.
10. Then he revealed to God's worshipper what was meant to be revealed.
11. He didn't disbelieve in what he saw.
12. Are you disputing what he saw?
13. Well, he saw him before.
14. By the tree (Sidrat Almuntaha) at the end of our domain.
15. Near the Garden of Refuge.
16. The Sidrat tree was covered with bright light.
17. His sight never wavered, nor was it too bold.
18. And he saw some of his Lord's greatest signs.
19. Tell me about Al-Lat and Al-Uzza
20. And Manat, the third one.
21. Are you to have the male, and he to have the female?
22. What a bad deal this is!
23. It's only names you invented with your fathers before. God did not authorize it. They only follow speculation and what their soul desires, even though guidance has come to them from their Lord.
24. Does human gets what he wishes?
25. To God belongs the end and the beginning.

26. How many angels in heaven whose petition will not be accepted until God gives permission to those He wants and accepts?
27. Those who do not believe in the end, they call angels by female names.
28. What knowledge do they have? They follow speculation, and speculation has no value against the truth.
29. Ignore those who turn away from Our revelation, who only want this lower life.
30. That's the most they achieved in knowledge. Your Lord knows who strays from His path and who follows His guidance.
31. To God belongs everything in the heavens and earth. He will punish those who did wrong with an equal amount, and He will reward those who did their best with better.
32. Those who avoid grave sins and forbidden sexual acts, except for the small ones, your Lord is a great forgiver. He knows you best as He produced you from the earth to the fetus stage in your mothers' wombs. So do not praise yourselves. He knows best who is mindful of Him.
33. Did you see the one who turns away?
34. He gave only a little, then stopped.
35. Does he have knowledge of the unseen, or does he see the future?
36. Has he not been told what was in Moses's scripture?
37. And of Abraham, who fulfilled his duty?
38. No one shall bear the burden of another.
39. Man will achieve only what he worked toward.
40. His fruits will be seen,
41. And he will be rewarded accordingly.
42. The final goal is your Lord—
43. He who makes you laugh and weep.
44. He who gives death and life.
45. He created the two genders, male and female,
46. From an ejected semen.
47. He will undertake the second creation.
48. He who gives wealth and possessions.
49. He is the Lord of the star Sirius.
50. He wiped out the first nation of Ad
51. And finished Thamud totally.

52. And before them, the people of Noah, who were even more unfair and oppressive.
53. He who brought down the Al Muatafika city (overturned city),
54. Covered by destruction.
55. Which of your Lord's blessings do you doubt?
56. This is a warning from the first warnings:
57. The end is near,
58. And only God knows when.
59. Are you shocked from this talk?
60. And you are laughing instead of crying?
61. You are clueless.
62. Forehead on the floor for God and worship.

Abasa (*Surah 80*)

1. He frowned and left
2. As the blind came to him.
3. Maybe he's ready to repent.
4. Or he could learn something useful.
5. But for the one that doesn't care,
6. You go out of your way.
7. What is it to you if he does not repent?
8. But the one who sought you out
9. And really cares,
10. You are distracted.
11. Indeed, it is a reminder
12. To whom wishes to remember
13. In the Holy Scripture's
14. Exalted, pure pages.
15. By the hands of ambassadors,
16. Noble and virtuous.
17. Woe to man! How ungrateful is he!
18. From what thing He created him?
19. From a droplet He started him, and then He proportioned him.
20. Then He pointed the way for him and made it easy.
21. Then He caused him to die and be buried.

22.When He wills, He will raise him up again.
23.Indeed, if he did not fulfill God's orders,
24.Let human look at his food.
25.We poured down water,
26.Then caused the soil to split open
27.To make the grain grow.
28.Grapes and vegetables.
29.Olive trees, date palms.
30.Luscious gardens.
31.Fruits and feed.
32.To benefit you and your livestock.
33.When the loud scream is heard,
34.That day, he will run away from his brother,
35.His mother, his father,
36.His wife, his children.
37.Each of them on that day will be absorbed in his own issues.
38.Some faces will be shining,
39.Smiling, and hoping for the best.
40.Other faces will be dusty,
41.Covered in darkness.
42.Those are the corrupt deniers.

Al Shams (*Surah 91*)

1. By the sun at its brightest time
2. And the moon that follows it,
3. The day that reveals it,
4. And the night that conceals it.
5. By the sky and how He built it,
6. And the earth how He spread it.
7. By the self and what aligns it,
8. Inspired its impurity and purity.
9. The one who cleanses it wins,
10. And the one who conceals it loses.
11. Thamud doubted, out of corruption and arrogance,
12. When the most wicked man among them rose to the task.

13. The messenger of God asked them to allow God's camel to drink.
14. They doubted him and crippled the camel. So their Lord punished them for their crime by flattening it,
15. And He does not fear the consequences.

Al-Burooj (*Surah 85*)

1. By the sky and its constellations,
2. By the promised day,
3. By the witness and what they witnessed,
4. Murdered were the people of the ditch.
5. The great fire,
6. They sat on it
7. To witness what was done to the believers.
8. They despised them because they believe in God the Mighty and Praiseworthy,
9. The one that owns heaven and earth. God witnesses everything.
10. Those who persecute the believers and don't repent, they will be punished in hell, and they will be burned.
11. For those who believe and do good, there will be gardens with flowing streams—that is the great success.
12. Your Lord's punishment is severe.
13. He who started life and will restore it again.
14. He is the Most Forgiving, the Most Loving.
15. With His glorious throne,
16. He does what He wants.
17. Have you heard the story of the soldiers?
18. Of Pharaoh and Thamud?
19. Yet the disbelievers are still in denial.
20. God knows what they are up to.
21. This is truly a glorious Quran,
22. Saved on a preserved tablet.

Al Tin (*Surah 95*)

1. By the fig and the olive,
2. By the evolving years,
3. By this safe town,
4. We create human in the best shape,
5. Then reduce him to the lowest of the low.
6. Except those who believe and do good, they will have boundless reward.
7. So what makes you deny your debt?
8. Isn't God the most precise judge?

Quraish (*Surah 106*)

1. What is familiar to Quraish?
2. They are familiar with the winter and the summer journey.
3. So let them worship the Lord of this house,
4. Who secured them against hunger and fear.

Al-Qaari'a (*Surah 101*)

1. The disaster.
2. What disaster?
3. Do you know what disaster?
4. When people will bc like scattered moths
5. And the mountains will be like spread-out wool.
6. Those whose scales weigh more
7. Will have a pleasant life.
8. But those whose scales weigh less
9. Will fall down in a deep pit.
10. What deep pit, you say?
11. It is the blazing fire.

Al-Zalzala (*Surah 99*)

1. When the earth is shaken by the earthquake,
2. When the earth throws out its burdens,
3. When humans wonder what's going on with it,
4. On that day, it will tell all its news
5. Of what your Lord has inspired it to do.
6. People will be discharged separately to see their deeds.
7. Whoever has done an atom of good will see it.
8. Whoever has done an atom of evil will see it.

Al-Qiyaama (*Surah 75*)

1. By the Day of Resurrection
2. And by the always-feeling-guilty soul,
3. Does human think We are not able to put his bones back together?
4. Indeed, We can even reshape his thumbprint.
5. Human wants to deny what's coming to him.
6. He is wondering if there will be a Resurrection Day.
7. When your vision is blurred
8. And the moon eclipsed,
9. When the sun and the moon are gathered together,
10. Human will say, on that day, there is no escape.
11. Truly, there is no refuge.
12. Their destination on that day is your Lord.
13. On that day, human will be aware of what he did and did not do.
14. Human is a clear witness against himself
15. Despite all the excuses he may present.
16. Don't rush to repeat it.
17. We will make sure it is collected and narrated.
18. So when We narrate it, follow its narration.
19. And then We will make it clear.
20. Truly, you love to have it now
21. And neglect what comes after.
22. Faces on that day are glowing,
23. Directly looking at their Lord.

24. Faces on that day are gloomy.
25. They realize a great disaster is upon them –
26. When the soul reaches the collarbone,
27. When asking "Any healers out there?"
28. When he realizes he is not coming back,
29. When his legs are wrapped together.
30. To your Lord, on that day, you will be taken.
31. He didn't believe and didn't pray.
32. He denied and turned away.
33. He walked back to his people with arrogance.
34. Woe upon you!
35. Then woe upon you.
36. Does man think he will be left alone without being questioned?
37. Was he not a sperm out of a drop?
38. Then he became a clinging, which was designed and shaped,
39. Fashioned into a pair of male and female.
40. Isn't he powerful enough to revive the dead?

Al-Humaza (*Surah 104*)

1. Woe to every backbiting slanderer,
2. The one that gathers money and counts it.
3. Does he think his money would make him live forever?
4. Indeed, he will be banished to the crushing blaze.
5. Do you know what the crushing blaze is?
6. It is the burning fire of God
7. That can see inside you,
8. And it is sealed over them
9. With towering columns.

Al-Mursalaat (*Surah 77*)

1. By the transporters of information,
2. Like a fast storm,
3. Spreading far and wide,

4. Dividing forcefully,
5. Dropping a reminder
6. As proof or a warning:
7. What you were promised is real.
8. When the stars are dimmed
9. And the sky is ripped.
10. When the mountains collapse
11. And the messengers are scheduled.
12. For which day they are scheduled,
13. The Day of Parting Away.
14. Do you know what the Day of Parting Away is?
15. It is the worst day for those who deny.
16. Did We not perish the first of them?
17. And so the last will follow.
18. That's how We deal with the guilty.
19. It is the worst day for those who deny.
20. Have We not created you from a simple fluid?
21. Which We held in a secure place
22. For a determined period?
23. We are determined, and We can.
24. It is the worst day for those who deny.
25. Did We not make the earth a vessel?
26. Alive and dead?
27. We made the high mountains as anchors and provided you with sweet water.
28. It is the worst day for those who deny.
29. Meet what you denied.
30. Go to three columns of shade.
31. No shade nor relief from flames you will find.
32. It is shooting out large sparks
33. As bright as copper.
34. It is the worst day for those who deny.
35. On that day, they will be speechless,
36. And they will be given no chance to offer any excuses.
37. It is the worst day for those who deny.
38. This is the final day, where We gathered you with the early ones.
39. If you have any powers to plot, show me.

40. It is the worst day for those who deny.
41. Those who were aware will enjoy cool shade springs
42. And any fruit they desire.
43. Enjoy eating and drinking as a reward for your actions.
44. That's how We reward excellence.
45. It is the worst day for those who deny.
46. Eat and enjoy shortly, you criminals.
47. It is the worst day for those who deny.
48. When they were told "Bow down," they did not.
49. It is the worst day for those who deny.
50. In what revelation, after this, will they believe?

Qaf (*Surah 50*)

1. Qaf and the glorious Quran.
2. But they were surprised that the warner emerged from among them, and the deniers say, "How strange!
3. "So if we die and we become dust, to return is unlikely."
4. We know what the earth reduces from them. We keep comprehensive records.
5. They denied the truth when it came to them. They are in a state of delusion.
6. Did they not look at the sky above them? How We built it and decorated it? Do you see any flaws?
7. We spread out the earth and placed anchors and grew in it each amazing pair
8. As evidence and a reminder for every worshipper who turns to God.
9. And We send down blessed water to grow with it gardens, fields of grain,
10. And tall palms with clusters of dates
11. As sustenance for everyone and revival to a dead town. Such as resurrection.
12. Before them, the people of Noah have denied. So did the people of Rass, Thamud,
13. Ad, Pharaoh, the Lot brothers,

14. The people of Ikat and the people of Tubba—each denied their messengers, so they deserve My threat.
15. Were We incapable with the first creation? Yet they doubt a second creation.
16. We created human. We know what his self whispers, and We are closer to him than his jugular vein.
17. As the receivers receive, one on his right, one on his left.
18. He does not utter a single word without being recorded.
19. When death creeps up, you will know it's time. That's what you were trying to escape.
20. When you hear the trumpets, you will know it's the day.
21. Each self will arrive with a driver and a witness.
22. You wear unaware, but today We have removed your veil, and your sight is sharp.
23. His accomplice will say, "I have an aggressor here."
24. Dump in hellfire every stubborn disbeliever
25. Who hindered goodness, is aggressive and suspicious.
26. The one that associates other gods with God. Drop him into severe torture.
27. His accomplice will say, "Lord, I did not make him transgress. He had already gone far astray."
28. Do not argue in My presence. I already gave you a warning.
29. My word will not be changed, and I am not unjust to My creation.
30. The day We ask, "Hellfire, are you full?" And it answers, "Is there more?"
31. Paradise will be brought close to the righteous. It will no longer be far.
32. This is what you were promised for every one that turns to God a recordkeeper.
33. To whoever fears Al-Rahman without seeing him, who comes before Him with a clear conscience.
34. Enter it in peace. This is the Day of Everlasting Life.
35. They will have all that they wish, and We have more.
36. How many generations have We wiped out before them? They were mightier than them. So search the land. Are there any saviors?
37. That is a reminder to whoever has a heart or listens closely and bears witness.

38. We created the skies, the earth, and everything in between. It took six days without exhaustion.
39. Be patient with what they say and praise and thank your Lord before sunrise and before sunset.
40. Praise him at night with your forehead on the floor (*sujud*).
41. Listen out for when the caller will call from a nearby place.
42. When they really hear the scream, they will come out from their graves.
43. We who give life and death—the final return will be to Us.
44. The day the earth will be torn apart, letting them rush out, gathering them will be easy for Us.
45. We know what they are saying, and you will not control them. So remind with the Quran those who fear My warning.

Al-Balad (*Surah 90*)

1. I swear by this town,
2. As you are part of this town,
3. And by a father and his offspring,
4. That We have created human with struggle.
5. Does he think that no one can overpower him?
6. He says, "I have spent a lot of money."
7. He thinks no one will see him.
8. Did We not give him eyes,
9. A tongue, and lips?
10. And pointed out to him the two ways?
11. He did not pass the obstacle.
12. Do you know what obstacle?
13. It is to free a slave.
14. Or to feed at a time of hunger
15. An orphaned relative
16. Or a poor person in distress.
17. And to be one of those who believe and urge patience and mercy.
18. Those are on the right.
19. And the ones that deny Our revelations will be damned.
20. Hellfire will lock over them.

Al-Alaq: Part 2

1. But human exceeds all boundaries
2. When he thinks he is self-sufficient.
3. You will return to your Lord.
4. Have you seen who forbids
5. A worshipper from praying?
6. Have you seen whether he is on the right path
7. Or encourages piety?
8. Have you seen him denying the truth and turning away?
9. Does he not realize that God sees all?
10. No, if he does not stop, We shall smack his forehead –
11. His lying, sinful forehead.
12. Let him summon his party.
13. We shall summon the guards of hell.
14. No! Do not obey him. Place your forehead on the floor and come close!

Al-Muddaththir: Part 2

1. Let me deal with the one I created alone,
2. Then gave him vast wealth
3. And sons by his side.
4. Made his life easy.
5. Yet he still asks for more.
6. He has been stubbornly hostile to Our revelation.
7. I will make it so bad for him.
8. He planned and plotted.
9. Damn his plot.
10. And again, damn his plotting.
11. Then he stared,
12. Frowned, and scowled
13. And turned away arrogantly.
14. He said, "This is just old sorcery.

15."Just the words of a mortal!"
16.He will burn in Saqar.
17.What is Saqar?
18.It spares nothing and leaves nothing.
19.It scorches the flesh of humans.
20.Nineteen are in charge of it.
21.None other than angels to guard hellfire; and We have their number, nineteen, to test the disbelievers. People of the book will be certain, and the believers will increase their belief. No doubt shall come to people of the book and the believers. The sick at heart and the disbelievers will say, "Why would God use this as an example?" That's how God allows whoever wants to go astray and whoever wants to be guided. No one knows your Lord's soldiers except Him. This is a reminder to mankind.
22.By the moon,
23.The departing night,
24.And the shining dawn,
25.It is one of the big ones –
26.A warning to all mortals,
27.To those of you who choose to go ahead or lag behind:
28.Every self is held by its deeds,
29.Except for those of the right.
30.In heaven, they are wondering
31.About the guilty.
32.What drove you to Saqar?
33.Their answer would be "We were not among the ones that pray.
34."We did not feed the poor.
35."We indulged with others in mocking.
36."We denied the Day of Judgment
37."Until the Certain End came upon us."
38.No intermediary will save them now.
39.What's wrong with them? Why do they turn away from the warning?
40.Just like wild zebras
41.Fleeing from a lion.
42.Each one of them wants his own scripture revealed.
43.They have no fear of the end.
44.Truly, it is a reminder

45. To whoever wishes to pay attention.
46. They would not remember unless God wishes. He is worthy of being obeyed, and He is capable of forgiveness.

Alqalam (*Surah 68*)

1. Nun, the pen and what they write.
2. You are not (with the blessings of your Lord) crazy.
3. You will have endless rewards.
4. You truly have the greatest character.
5. Soon, you will see, as will they,
6. Which of you is the insane.
7. Your Lord knows better who strays from His path and who is guided.
8. Do not obey the liars.
9. They want you to compromise, and then they will compromise.
10. Do not obey the despicable swearer.
11. Backbiter, slanderer.
12. Obstructor of good, sinful, aggressive.
13. Mean, rough, and, on top of all that, envious
14. In spite of his money and buildings.
15. When he hears Our revelation recited, he says, "It's just fairy tales."
16. We shall brand him on the snout!
17. We have tested them as We tested the owners of the garden, who swore that they would harvest it in the morning,
18. Disregarding God's will.
19. A disaster from your Lord struck it while they were sleeping.
20. By the morning, it was stripped bare.
21. They called each other at daybreak.
22. "Leave early if you wish to gather all its fruits."
23. And they went off, whispering,
24. "Make sure no poor person enters the garden today,"
25. Determined to achieve their goal.
26. When they saw it, they said, "We must have lost our way.
27. "We are ruined."
28. The wisest of them said, "Didn't I tell you to glorify?"

29.They said, "Glory to our Lord! Truly, we were doing wrong."
30.Then they turned on each other in blame.
31.They said, "We are in trouble. We overdid it.
32."May our Lord replace it with something better. We truly turn to Him in hope."
33.Such is the punishment, but greater still is the punishment in the hereafter. If only they knew.
34.For those who are mindful of God, blessed gardens. Are the criminals equal to the submitters?
35.What's wrong with you? On what basis do you judge?
36.Or do you have an alternative book that you're learning from?
37.And you have in it all your wishes.
38.Or you have from Us a binding contract, till Resurrection Day, that you can get whatever you want?
39.Ask them which of them can claim that.
40.Or if they have "partners," let them produce their "partners" if what they say is true.
41.When the calamity comes, they will be asked to put their foreheads on the floor, but they can't.
42.Their eyes will be downcast with humility as they had the chance to do so when it was safe.
43.Leave Me with the deniers of this event. We shall lead them on without them knowing.
44.I will allow them more time, for My plan is powerful.
45.Do We demand some reward from them that would burden them with debt?
46.Do they have knowledge of the unseen that enables them to share what's going to happen?
47.Wait patiently for your Lord's judgment. Do not be like the man of the whale who called out in distress.
48.If his Lord's grace had not reached him, he would have been left abandoned on the barren shore.
49.But his Lord chose him and made him one of the righteous.
50.The disbelievers almost strike you down with their looks when they hear the revelation. They say, "He must be mad!"
51.It is only a reminder for both worlds.

Al-Taariq (*Surah 86*)

1. The skies and the Night Visitor,
2. Do you know what the Night Visitor is?
3. It's the piercing star.
4. Each soul has a guardian.
5. Human should look into what he was created from.
6. He is created from a gushing fluid
7. That emerges from vessels underneath the bladder.
8. God is certainly able to bring him back to life.
9. The day when secrets are out,
10. He will have no power and no one to help him.
11. The sky and its recurring clouds.
12. The earth and those cracks.
13. It's a decisive statement.
14. It is not to be taken lightly.
15. They plot and scheme.
16. And so do I.
17. Let the disbelievers be. Let them be for a while.

Al-Qamar (*Surah 54*)

1. As the hour draws near, the moon will split.
2. As they see the sign, they say, "Same old sorcery!"
3. They reject the truth and follow their own desires. Everything stays the same.
4. They have received enough notice to restrain them,
5. Far-reaching wisdom, but the warnings did not help.
6. Turn away from them. When the caller will call to that horrific event,
7. Eyes downcast, they will come out of their graves like swarming locusts.
8. Rushing to the caller, the disbelievers will cry, "This is a harsh day!"
9. Before them, people of Noah denied the truth. They rejected Our worshipper, saying, "He is mad!" and scolded him.
10. He called upon his Lord, "I am defeated. Help me!"
11. So We opened the gates of the sky with torrential rain.

12. Burst the earth with gushing springs. All met for a predetermined purpose.
13. We carried him along on a vessel of timber tied together
14. That floated under Our watchful eye as a punishment to the deniers.
15. We have left this as a sign. Will anyone remember?
16. How terrible My punishment was, and how I fulfilled My threat!
17. We have made it easy to learn Quran. Will anyone remember?
18. The people of Ad also denied. How terrible My punishment was, and how I fulfilled My threat!
19. We released a howling wind against them on a day of terrible disaster.
20. It swept people away like uprooted palm trunks.
21. How terrible My punishment was, and how I fulfilled My threat!
22. We have made it easy to learn Quran. Will anyone r remember?
23. The people of Thamud also rejected the warnings.
24. They said, "Are we supposed to follow one man from among us? That would be misguided. Quite insane!
25. "He received the revelation alone from among us? No, he is an arrogant liar!"
26. Tomorrow they will know who the arrogant liar is.
27. We are sending the camel to test them, so watch and be patient.
28. Tell them the water is to be shared with the camel. They drink when their turn comes.
29. But they called their companion, who took a sword and crippled the camel.
30. How terrible My punishment was, and how I fulfilled My threat!
31. We released a single mighty blast against them, and they ended up like dry sticks.
32. We have made it easy to learn Quran. Will anyone remember?
33. The people of Lot denied the warnings.
34. We released a storm of stones on them, all except the family of Lot. We saved them before dawn
35. As a blessing from Us. This is how We reward the thankful.
36. He warned them of Our destruction, but they dismissed the warning.
37. They insisted on taking his guests, so We sealed their eyes. "Taste My punishment and My threat!"

38. Very early in the morning, they received an ongoing punishment until they perished.
39. Taste My punishment and My threat!
40. We have made it easy to learn Quran. Will anyone remember?
41. The people of Pharaoh also received warnings.
42. They denied all Our signs, so We took them on with Our might and power.
43. Are your deniers any better than these? Or have you an exemption in the scripture?
44. Or they will say, "We have greater numbers. We will win."
45. But they will lose and flee.
46. And when the time comes, it will be more severe and bitter on them.
47. The criminals will have great hardship.
48. They will be dragged on their faces in hell. "Feel the touch of hell."
49. Everything We created is measured.
50. We only have to say it once. It will happen in the blink of an eye.
51. We have destroyed the likes of you in the past. Will anyone remember?
52. Everything they did is recorded in the books.
53. Every action, great or small, is written.
54. The alert will be in gardens and rivers,
55. Sitting in a truthful seat with the Most Capable King.

Saad (*Surah 38*)

1. Saad and the easy-to-remember Quran.
2. Yet the deniers are steeped in arrogance and hostility.
3. How many generations did We destroy before them? It's too late for them.
4. They think it strange that the warner is from among them. They say, "He is just a lying sorcerer!
5. "He is claiming there is only one God. What an astonishing thing to claim!"
6. Their leaders walk away, saying, "Stay faithful to your gods! This was planned.

7. "We did not hear any such claim in the last doctrine. It is all an invention.
8. "Was the message sent only to him out of all of us?" In fact, they doubt My warning. In fact, they have not tasted My punishment yet.
9. Do they possess the treasures of your Lord's bounty, the Mighty, the All-Giving?
10. Do they control the heavens and earth and everything between? Let them climb their ropes.
11. Their armed alliance is weak and will be crushed. Their alliance army have lost already.
12. The people of Noah, Ad, and the Pharaoh of the Pyramids denied before them.
13. Thamud, the people of Lot, and the forest dwellers—they are the opposition.
14. They all rejected the messengers, and they all deserve My punishment.
15. All they are waiting for is a single blast that cannot be stopped.
16. They say, "Our Lord! Give us our share of punishment before the Day of Judgment!"
17. Be patient with what they say and remember Our worshipper David, a man of strength who always obeys.
18. We made the mountains join him in glorifying Us at sunset and sunrise.
19. Flocks of birds all obey him.
20. We strengthened his kingdom. We gave him wisdom and a decisive way of speaking.
21. Have you heard the news of the two opponents who climbed into his private quarters?
22. As they reached David, he got nervous. But they said, "Do not be afraid. We are two opponents, one of whom has wronged the other. Judge between us fairly. Do not be unjust and guide us to the right path."
23. "This is my brother. He had ninety-nine ewes, and I, just the one. He said, 'Let me take charge of her,' and overpowered me with his words."
24. David said, "He has done you wrong by demanding to add your ewe to his flock. Many partners treat each other unfairly. Those who

believe and do good deeds do not do this, but these are very few." David realized that We are testing him. So he asked his Lord for forgiveness, fell down to his knees, and repented.

25.So We forgave him that. He is close to Us, and he has a great future.

26.David, We have appointed you a successor over land. Judge between people rightfully. Do not follow your desires. They will divert you from God's path. Those who wander from His path will have a painful torment because they ignore Judgment Day.

27.We did not create heaven, earth, and everything in between without a purpose. That's what the disbelievers assume. How they will suffer from the fire.

28.Would We make those who believe and do good and those who spread corruption on earth equal? Would We make those who follow God's direction as those who are recklessly wicked?

29.This book that We have sent down to you is blessed, for people to think about its verses and for those with intelligence to remember.

30.We blessed David with Solomon. He was a great worshipper who always turned to God.

31.When high-stepper horses were paraded before him near the end of day,

32.My love of fine things kept me away from remembering my Lord until they disappeared from sight!

33."Bring them back!" And he started to stroke their legs and necks.

34.We tested Solomon by dropping a body on his throne. Then he repented.

35.He said, "Lord, forgive me! Grant me such power as no one after me will have. You are the greatest Provider."

36.So We gave him power over the wind, which, at his request, ran gently wherever he wished.

37.And the devils, every kind of builder and diver.

38.And others, chained in shackles.

39.This is Our gift. So give or withhold as you wish without an account.

40.His reward will be closeness to Us and a good place to return to.

41.In memory of Our worshipper Job, who called on his Lord, "Satan has caused me pain and suffering."

42.Stamp your foot! Here is cool water for you to wash and drink.

43.We restored his family to him with many more like them—a sign of Our mercy and a lesson to all who understand.
44.Take a small bunch of grass and strike her with that so as not to break your oath. We found him patient. An excellent worshipper, he always turned to God.
45.In memories of Our worshippers, Abraham, Isaac, and Jacob all had strength and vision.
46.We caused them to be sincerely remembered in this life.
47.With us, they are among the best of the best.
48.And in memories of Our worshippers, Ishmael, Elisha, and Dhu Al-Kifl were among the best.
49.This is a reminder. The aware will have a good place to return to.
50.The gates of lasting gardens will be open for them,
51.They will be lounging with a lot of fruits and drinks.
52.They will have modest gaze companions.
53.This is what you are promised for the Day of Judgment.
54.Our sustenance for you will never end.
55.But the extremist will have the worst place to return to:
56.Hell to burn in. That's the worst destiny.
57.Let them taste it boiling and bitter cold
58.And other such torments.
59.Another crowd will enter. No "hello." No "welcome." Just "You will burn in hell."
60.They replied, "You're not welcome either. You brought this on us. It was a bad decision."
61.Adding, "Our Lord, give double punishment to those who brought this upon us.
62."How come we don't see certain men we considered evil
63."And used to make fun of? Have our eyes missed them?"
64.These are for sure the arguments of people of hell.
65.Say, "I am giving you a warning. There is no god, but God. The One, the All-Powerful.
66."Lord of the heavens and earth and everything between, the Almighty, the Most Forgiving."
67.Say, "It's the greatest news,
68."Yet you ignore it.
69."I had no knowledge of the argument at the highest realms of power.

70.“What’s revealed to me is that I am here to give a clear warning.”
71.Your Lord said to the angels, “I am creating mankind from mud.
72.“So when he is fully developed and connected to My spirit, fall down and kneel before him.”
73.All the angels kneeled down together,
74.Except for Iblis, who was too proud and rejected.
75.“Iblis, what prevents you from kneeling down to what I have created with My own hands? Are you too high and mighty?”
76.Iblis said, “I am better than him. You created me from fire and created him from mud.”
77.“Get out of here! You are cast out!
78.“My curse will follow you till Payback Day.”
79.Iblis said, “My Lord, allow me to live until Resurrection Day.”
80.He said, “You are among those who will live.
81.“Till the Appointed Day.”
82.Iblis said, “I swear by Your might! I will tempt them,
83.“Except for your loyal worshippers.”
84.He said, “This is the truth—I speak only the truth.
85.“I will fill hell with you and all those that follow you.”
86.Say, “I ask no reward from you for this, nor do I claim to be what I am not.”
87.It’s only a reminder for both worlds,
88.And you will learn its news later.

End of

Book One
Before Religion

Coming Soon

Book Two
Real Religion

For more information, contact

Yassir Rousan
yassirrousan@gmail.com

www.ingramcontent.com/pod-product-compliance
Lightning Source LLC
Chambersburg PA
CBHW080534030426
42337CB00023B/4736

* 9 7 9 8 2 1 8 8 8 7 5 7 5 *